THE YEAR OF THE HORSE

Other Books by the Author:

THE YEAR OF THE HORSE

A Book of Poems and Prophecies

By

ELLIS OVESEN

THE GOLDEN QUILL PRESS
Publishers
Francestown   New Hampshire

Library of Congress Catalog Card Number 90-85826

ISBN 0-8233-0472-8

Printed in the United States of America

This book is dedicated to Dr. Richard G. Collmer, Director of "THE HOUSE OF POETRY" at Baylor University, Waco, Texas. His constant encouragement and perceptive insight have been a great inspiration to me.

This book is also dedicated to my son, Theo, whose constant companionship and help has sustained me.

The Author wishes to thank all of the presses in the United States of America and abroad who have published her work.

Wyndham Hall Press recently published *The Year of the Snake* and republished *The Flowers of God*. *Beloved* was published this year in a new format by Chetana Books of Mangalore, India.

Do Not Go Away was recently published by Plowman Press of Canada.

CONTENTS

THE YEAR OF THE HORSE

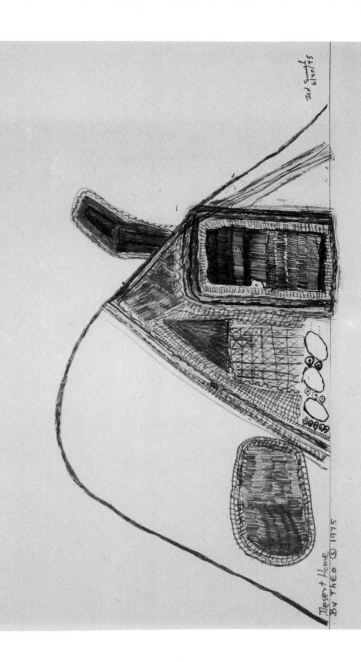

Desert Home
By THEO © 1975

THE FOUR HORSEMEN

The four horsemen:
    has anybody seen them
    grinding the earth
    with savage maw?

The four horsemen:
    has anybody seen them
    treading the grapes
    with dreadful paw?

The off-white horse
    of the false church:
    its rider carrying the Cupid's Bow of human and
    false love.

The red horse
    of war,
    its rider sowing seeds of dissatisfaction and ill
    will.

The black horse
    of plague,
    its rider carrying AIDS, cancer and old-world and
    new-world disease.

The pale horse
    of death and famine,
    its rider starving the little children with
    protruding bellies.

After this, will Come the True White Horse
of the Faithful and True:
The Sword of its Rider will pierce through soul
and spirit,
The Sword of the Prince of Peace,
Jesus of Nazareth, the Messiah!
Hallelujah!

ORPHEUS

When Orpheus strummed
    his Golden Lyre,
He could the *coldest* rock inspire,
    the sun prolong . . .

The nightingale no sweeter note
    could cause to utter from its throat
    than Orpheus Song!

For when he sang,
    the winds stood still;
    the oceans listened with a will;
    the snow and ice forgot to chill;
    All things surrendered to his skill...
    when Orpheus Sang!

I wish that I as well expressed
Emotions surging in *my* breast
    beyond control!

How eagerly I would explore
the mysteries of hidden Lore
    that Clothe the Soul:

I, too, the winds' bold blast would kill;
I, too, the seas with awe instill:
My melody would quite fulfill
    Hope's fondest Dream!

"KRYSTALLNACHT"

They bottle-bombed our home
    On "the night of flying glass;"
And gave my husband
    A glass of poisoned wine . . .
On "the night of flying glass,"
    They smashed the synagogue
And boarded up the buildings
    On the block . . .

They killed our airedale guard-dog
    On "the night of flying glass;"
And tore the kittens
    From our tabby's womb.
On "the night of flying glass,"
    The sun turned black as coal
And the moon was red with
    Jew and Christian blood.

They crucified our tom
    On "the night of flying glass,"
And placed a crown of thorns
    Upon his head:
On "the night of flying glass,"
    A Holocaust of Bones
Rose up to Fight again
    The Nazi horde.

They cracked the Challenger
     On "the night of flying glass;"
And leavened the bread of Chernobyl
     With poisoned dust . . .
On "the night of flying glass,"
     "Ariane" fled to the heavens
And the LAKE OF FIRE
     Reached up to grasp her flames . . .

Messiah Flew through the Gate
     On "the night of flying glass";
The Sword of Longiness Cut
     Through True from false.
On "the night of flying glass",
     The Angels Sang again
For the Birth of a New Earth . . .
     And JERUSALEM CAME DOWN!

PALM SUNDAY

He came upon a donkey, the humblest of all beasts:
To the sound of loud "hosanna's"
By his disciples, released
To the thought that a man named Jesus
Is King of all the Jews
Because he Healed, Raised from the dead . . .
They *shouted* out the news!

But other men were watching
And they did not approve;
They did not want a ragged man . . .
They asked the group to move . . .
They wanted then to kill him, as they had
    wished before . . .
He had no education
Nor knowledge of their written lore.

His message was too simple;
His lifestyle was too lean . . .
"Give Love to one another;
Forgive, treat no one mean."

And, so they crucified him
Upon a splintery tree
And took away his cloak:
He had no money.

Now, people stand in prayer:
They know what they have missed.
But He is Coming back again
For others on the *List*.

16

The Rapture will be Glorious . . .
The ragamuffin scene:
They cannot walk: they cannot talk:
They *Sing with Spirits Keen* . . .

"Were you there?" their hearts are crying;
"Do you Know Him?" their eyes shout:
"Let me tell you about Jesus . . .
Let me heal your inner doubt."

"Let me tell you about Jesus,"
Sings the ragamuffin clan;
And the world turns back its hooded eye
And draws another crucifixion plan . . .

But they never quite can catch Him
For His Gold cannot be bought . . .
It is Truth that makes Him Live:
Love, Forgiveness, as He taught.

I AM BUYING HIM A NEW JACKET

I am buying him a new jacket
To replace his dirty, food-stained old one . . .
"These are his little Treasures," the clerk
    smiles gently,
As she pulls out the dust balls; the smashed
    bottle caps and cans;

The old candy bar wrappers . . .
Other people's discarded mail and Christmas cards . . .
He gets no mail of his own.

Someone had stolen his wallet the day before,
Bulging with picked-up address cards;
Containing two dollars.

Someone had stolen his notebook a year before
With the numbering, descending songs of his
    waning mind . . .

Someone wants his SSI check . . .
So they can put him into a black hole and forget him.

They will steal even the dust balls and the discarded
    Christmas cards . . .

He is past forty: and no one sings in the dark anymore;
No school bells or church bells ring . . .
No one brings a candle to supplement the fading
    electricity of his house . . .

A little match girl sits in a darkened corner, smiling,
She, alone, has Faith.

FOR THE SPOTTED OWL, ETC.

My nest is gone:
    The bulldozer did its reaping
When all my little
    Sweetie-lumps were sleeping . . .
They're tearing up the places
    Where we breed,
Pretending to protect us
    While they feed
On redwood stumps which
    Once we had for homes . . .
Alas! Alas! We once knew
    Sheltered domes
Among the lovely redwoods
    Now strewn dead . . .
Will there be only one tree left,
    As the President said?*

*"When you've seen one tree
  you've seen 'em all" . . .
      (President Ronald Reagan)

ON FATHER'S DAY

I love that old man in there,
Peein' on mother's shawl;
Feedin' orange juice to the cat:
Paintings from Van Gogh magazines on his wall.

He once dressed sharp and fine;
Built beautiful wood cabinets—
But after three sudden deaths,
He lies in the bed and wets.

He used to love his home;
He built it all himself;
But tragedy was too much;
And now he is on life's shelf.

A man of love and joy—
He "managed" everything . . .
All of a sudden he's gone . . .
No matter what I sing;

No matter what I say,
It does not bring him back;
The mind is a fragile thing;
I grieve for what I lack.

And so I smile at him
And try to keep him warm;
For life is a fragile thing;
And age is a wild snowstorm.

I love that old man in there
Who's peein' in the bed,
The memories and joys
Of what he once was, fled.

I love that old man in there,
Who's peein' in his bed;
And I will always love him
Because *my* life he fed.

He fed it with love and laughter;
He fed it with joy and hope.
My life had a joy of childhood
Because he was my Pope.

We sang and danced together;
And life was good and glad . . .
I am proud to say I can claim him
As my *wonderful, precious Dad!*

(Happy Father's Day, Dad,
Wherever you are!)

THE FIELDS

He's in the fields right now
                Tending the sheep;
He often helps his father
                With the wood.

I keep a bare-swept floor . . .

The bag of meal
                in the corner
Is for our breakfast dish—

A sweet, sweet child;
I love him dearly;
But I do not always understand
                The things he says—

"I must do my *Father's* bidding,"
He tells me softly;
He dreams a lot
And smiles at me *so* tenderly,
                Seeming to be anxious for *my* joy:

"Someday you will understand,"
He says.
I am distressed . . .
And yet there is a Peace
                I can't explain.

He's very giving—
I've watched him playing
With the other children, and
He lets *them* take the lead—

He does not like
To see distress in any Creature . . .

I keep a clean-swept floor . . .
There are many things
I do not understand. . .

THERE ARE NO CHRISTMAS TREES
IN BETHELEHEM THIS YEAR

There are no Christmas trees in Bethlehem this year:
The lights are out upon the commercialized creche.
The Cross looms stark and bare upon Golgotha's hill;
There are no Christmas trees in Bethlehem this year.

There are no Christmas trees in Bethlehem this year:
The streets are being swept and washed each night
In preparation for the Coming of the Messiah;
There are no Christmas trees in Bethlehem this year.

There are no Christmas trees in Bethlehem this year:
Santa Claus and his sleigh have departed for parts
    unknown.
Only the Cross is welcome from now on;
There are no Christmas trees in Bethlehem this year.

There are no Christmas trees in Bethlehem this year:
There is no Sunday worship.
The False Church is now banned.
There are no Christmas trees in Bethlehem this year.

There are no Christmas trees in Bethlehem this year:
The occult and Satan worshippers;
The astrologers are gone.
There are no Christmas trees in Bethlehem this year.

There are no Christmas trees in Bethlehem this year:
Trees are growing *live* on the Mount of Olives where
    He prayed.

Ted Smith.
6/14/75

Sheep graze upon the grasses; angels are singing in
the sky.

There are no Christmas trees in Bethlehem this year.

JEREMIAH 10:3-4: "For the customs of the people are
vain: for one cutteth a tree out of the forest . . . They deck
it with silver and gold, they fasten it with nails and with
hammers, that it move not."

THE LITTLE HERMIT THRUSH

The little hermit thrush
    always comes to my back yard
      at Christmas-time
    to make her
nest . . .

I never see her
      nest;
I never see her
      mate . . .

She flitters among the
    shadows
      of the
    leaves,
      hunting
    food
      for her
    family.

I am
    overjoyed
      to see her
    return
      every Christmas-time
    to my back yard
    to start the Year
Anew!

HELEN C. WHITE

Helen C. White, PhD,
   Professor of English at the University of Wisconsin,
   always wore
Purple . . .

    We were told she'd been blessed by the
Pope:
       —a penitent pilgrim—
       who wrote books about
Saint Francis of Assisi—
       Builder for Peace—

Always a line of students
       in front of her office door,
       seeking help with their problems . . .

The GI's during the winter of World War II—
       (when I was a student
       at the University
       and she was my Advisor),

       slicked the snow to make an
ice slide down
Bascom Hill—
       so they could cheer the coeds from the sidelines,
       hoping some would fall . . .
       revealing lace panties . . .

I don't believe that
    Helen C. White, PhD, ever
slipped—

    She came into class one
morning
    and said, with that warm
twinkle in her eyes,

    "What they did not
know was,
    I was praying those
GI's would spend
    Purgatory sliding down that slippery, icy
slide!"

FOR HENRY

He has a girl friend; and her name is Rose:
He takes her with him everywhere he goes . . .
He writes a poem about her every night
And puts it in his pocket, where it Glows
With Blessèd Radiance and Holy Light . . .
He sees her in his travels, in the smiles
Of women whom he meets across the miles
He needs must travel in his walk through life—
And, though he never took a loving wife—
He's happy and he smiles because he knows
He has a girl friend; and her name is Rose.

COUCH POTATO

He fell asleep
        watching the Game:
Watching the Game
        did him in . . .

After a while
        he failed
To brush his teeth
        or comb his hair.

And then he wouldn't eat:
        he just drank beer
He fell asleep
        watching the Game:

Watching the Game
        did him in!

I WILL NEVER FORGET YOU, ROSALINA

I will never forget you, Rosalina:
You came, laughing, to help my son
When there was no one else to help . . .

Beautiful and black, you came
Singing, where there was no song . . .
You came,
Dancing, where there was no dance . . .

I have never known such Love as this upon the
   earth . . .
Such unselfish, giving Love.

You brought yellow flowers on my birthday . . .
So many kinds of yellow flowers.
I did not know there were so many kinds of yellow
   flowers:

There were daylilies and daisies;
And buttercups and poppies;
And daffodils and tulips;
And marigolds and snapdragons;

There were honeysuckle and jessamine;
Chrysanthemum and violets;
Spanish broom and pansies;
And iris and the rose.

You came out of *your* hell . . .
To cool *my* private hell of illness and distress . . .

31

I will never forget you, Rosalina.
You brought a new Vision of Jesus into my life . . .
You gave yourself
When no one else would.

You are God's pure and lovely black Angel
Dancing on the earth . . .
A ray of joy and peace
In a disappearing, crumbling world . . .

You are black and I am white:
What can I give to you to match your Perfect Gift?

I will never forget you,
Rosalina.

FOR EDNA MEUDT

At five, she killed five rattlesnakes
To buy her Dad a birthday gift;
But when her Daddy found this out,
He was *really* miffed.

He said, "Now, don't you ever do that
Again, my Edna, dear;
For I don't need a gift so much
As I need to have *you near!*"

FOR TUCK ABOUT TO RETIRE

Now, she will keep her closets clean;
And she will tend her pansy bed . . .
She'll sweep the oak leaves from her walk:
Her dog, her cat, will be well fed.

But I will miss her cluttered desk,
The papers falling to the floor . . .
She's sitting in a rocking chair,
She's mending aprons—what a bore!

I will not have the time to call . . .
My floors unswept, my beds unmade:
Another deadline lies ahead . . .
She's waltzing in The Promenade!

Perhaps we'll meet Someplace, Somewhere
In some old far-off Fountained Square
And have a Cup of Tea for two . . .
Write what you want: "THE MOON IS BLUE!"

FOR JOY

Now that Beth is dead,
Another hill of pain is
Waiting to be climbed.

WAS THERE A DAY?

Was there a day I should have said, "Please stay."
To a friend, who, misunderstanding, walked away?
Was there a day I should have said, "Come back!"
To a child, who, trembling, left with his backpack?
Was there a day I should have said, "I love you."
To a beau who ran away with skies of blue?
Was there a day I could have made one wise
Who cringed under a false flag of lies?
I was building this Temple for you, my friend;
This Day is Now: it soon will end.

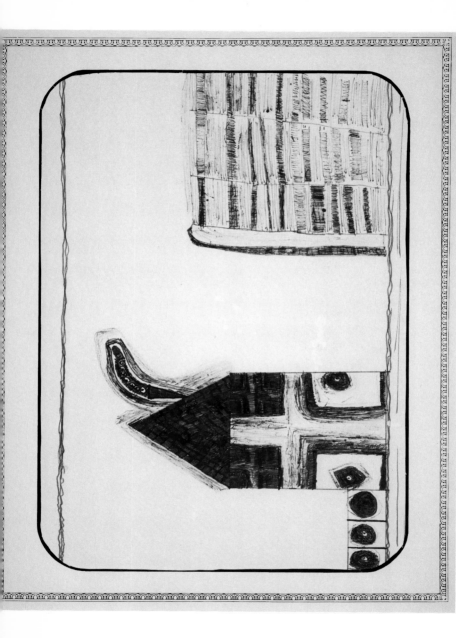

FOR JERRY

He stumbled as he read his poem, blue against the day.
"I was just a little boy when they took my Mom away:
They say my Mom is crazy; but I love her anyway."

"They say my Mom is crazy; but I love her anyway . . .
They used to say, 'Now, Jerry, just run outside and
    play . . .' "
He stumbled as he read his poem, blue against the day.

He stumbled as he read his poem, blue against the day.
"Sometimes she'd sit and chatter to me like a bloomin'
    jay . . .
They say my Mom is crazy; but I love her anyway . . ."

"One night I was beside her bed; all night long I lay . . .
To hear her laugh and chatter; to listen to her pray."
He stumbled as he read his poem, blue against the day . . .
"They say my Mom is crazy; but I love her anyway."

FOR EDWIN FALKOWSKI—
A MEMORIAL HAIKU

Squinting at the Light,
He said, "I have nothing left
To Give . . .but this Flame."

EARTHQUAKE OF OCTOBER 17, 1989

An antique cup flies off the mantle . . .
I sink into the sofa . . .
It is my first earthquake . . .

It is over in a few seconds . . .
And then the scattered reports come in . . .
San Francisco the Marina, Watsonville, Los Gatos,
   Aptos, Santa Cruz . . .

The Golden Gate—a symbol of joy and light—
Not like the cold, dark chasms of New York—

We have been told The Big One is coming . . .

Everyone knows the earth is wearing out.
Everyone knows we are in our last drag race.
There are worms in every fish: oil and pollution in
   every sea.

Hey, how about buying a ten acre spread on Mars—
   or on the Moon—for $10 or $20?
That is, if you've got $10 or $20 to spare—
   See you there . . .

And, in the meantime,

There is another Golden Gate beyond the sea—
It is even more Glamorous,
   Bejewelled with Sapphire and Pearl and Emerald
   and Ruby!

BIG STONE LAKE

In spring, we kids would leap from stone to stone
Along the shores of beautiful Big Stone Lake,
Looking for Indian hammers,
Pushed up by winter ice.

This lake had once been home to Big Sioux Indians,
Who fished and made flint arrowheads for game.

One spring, we found a lovely coral pendant,
Hand manufactured from some kind of shell—
Once worn by an Indian Princess, so we thought...

We dreamed of evening trysts in a canoe
At sunset, with the water lapping low;
An evening star:
A kiss of promise made.

Those days of woodland paradise are gone . . .
Gone is our childhood by this lovely lake,
Where Indians long before had found its Song.

IT'S APRIL IN CALIFORNIA

It's April in California:
And everything's in bloom!
The rose, the pyracantha
And the Spanish broom!

The apricot, the cherry,
The walnut and the prune;
Ceanothus and azalea,
And "Lilies of the Moon."

My nose is raw and bleeding;
I look like a baboon:
I'm taking antihistamines
And vitamins by the spoon.

It's April in California:
I can hardly wait for June.
It's April in California . . .
And everything's in bloom!

THE GENTLE HEART

Oh, who will mend
    the gentle heart
Caught in a restless
    sleep?
The gentle heart is bleeding
    to an alcoholic beat . . .

Her husband found another
    and left her
        ill and old:
    and now she sleeps
Beneath a shawl
    to keep her from the cold . . .

Her husband took their
    only child
For jealousy and spite . . .
And now she has no one to love
To keep her Soul a-Light . . .

Oh, do I see a letter . . .
Hear a ringing on the phone?
Is someone there to hold her
    hand:
To soften pain and moan?

Oh, who will mend the
    gentle heart
So broken; once complete . . .
Oh, who will mend the gentle heart
With the alcoholic beat?

42

HOME

Home is where I do *not* want to be:
A fever in my blood says, "Run! . . .Run Free . . .
Along a mountain track or by the sea:
Flee with the gulls into the sunset sky!
Fly with the clouds into the gentle night!
Don't stand there hoeing corn and pulling weeds:
Watch how the dewdrops spin their little beads:
Follow the rainbow arced with colors bright!
Go where the storm drops feather . . .fly! fly! fly!

LOVE SINGS IN THE AFTERGLOW

Love Sings in the Afterglow
Of every argument . . .
After each sweet lament,
Love Sings in the Afterglow,

I wake to hear you crying—
No one has paid the rent—
Why do we stay to find
What it was the other meant?

Love Sings in the Afterglow
Of every argument . . .
After each sweet lament,
Love Sings in the Afterglow . . .

PAPER BOY

There he is
    Huffing over his
        Bike:
He has thrown my
    paper and
        Gone . . .
And I am too late again . . .
    Because I am old . . .
        And not fast enough . . .
To greet him with
    My little gift of
        Thanks!

FOR CRAIG

They have moved his table and chair
Out onto the parking lot—
Where he sat eating bread and drinking milk
At lunchtime—

He was there yesterday, laughing
In his black stocking cap—
Trying to explain the sun
And the equinox.

My friend in Del Mar
Had slept on a town bench for years . . .
Obscured by some bushes . . .

Someone nailed a 2 x 4 upright
In the middle of the bench
While painting their store . . .

Spikes sticking up.

I nailed down the spikes,
But could not remove the board.

An old man in town
Brought his donkey and dog,
Dressed up for fiesta;
Tails braided and ribboned . . .

They were kicked out . . .

No good for business . . .

I came just to see them.

Craig is a veteran—
Won the Purple Heart in the Vietnam War
I would have fled for Canada to escape—
Did my fighting for me—
Lost his mind—
Now, he can fight no more . . .

"THE ROSE OF CASTILE"

Bloody footprints marked the adobe
of Father Junipero Serra's Mission Trail:
in spite of bleeding feet,
the little priest
"with the heart of a lion" . . .
walked on . . .

At the end of the trail,
Juan Rodrîguez Cabrillo
called Father Serra to his tent:
"Father Serra,"
Juan said,
"I want to ask your blessing:
I have had many blessings
but I especially covet yours."

"Father in Heaven,"
said Serra,
"May *all* who come this way be
Blessed; and *all* who
inhabit this beautiful,
Wonderful
land."

YOUR LOVES ARE MINE

When I am gone,
my love will still be here,
hovering over the
leafsills,
covering you like a
shrine.

When I am gone,
the energy
released
will sing in suspended
circles,
haloing your mind.

For what is love
but back to its
beginnings,
shining in sirening
splendor to the
dawn?

And what is love
but a flock of wild
birds in springtime . . .
I will not leave you,
for your loves are
mine.

THE FACE OF ULTIMATE EVIL

I have looked upon the face of ultimate evil—
It is expressionless:
It has no conscience . . .
It is inhabited by demons.

It strips the skin from little children,
Letting their blood drip.
It tapes their mouths
So no one hears their screams.

It eats their inner organs—
And drinks their blood,
Consecrating them to Satan.

It melts their fat in vats;
And tears their hair for Nazi children's toys.

It trains its slaves and animals to vicious crimes,
Giving them cocaine and other mind-destroying drugs.

It feeds their parents sausage ground from the flesh
Of its own children . . .
It tries in every way to destroy the Soul
As well as the body.

The Nazi Party of Adolf Hitler is
The face of ultimate evil,
Trying to conquer the Universe by terror:
It wants nothing to live but itself.

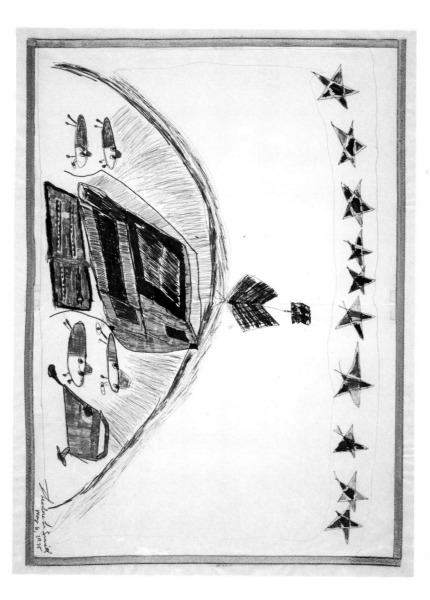

It wears a black mustache
And a pickerel smile.
It wears a drooping forelock
Over one eye.

There was another man who walked the earth—
He showed us how to defeat this most evil Devil
And throw him into the Lake of Fire,
Where the Beast and False Prophet
And their followers
Also will be thrown.

I HEAR THE CHILDREN
CRYING ALL OVER THE WORLD

I hear Muammar al-Qaddafi's children
   crying after the missile hit their
      home.

I hear the starving Ethiopian children
   crying for their
      food.

I hear the children of Brazil,
   gunned down in the
      streets.

I hear the latch key children
   of the United States of
      America.

I hear the Romanian children
   naked in their
      orphanage.

I hear the culted Christian children
   being eaten
      alive.

I hear the PLO children,
   bones broken with large
      stones.

I hear the children crying,
    whose parents have AIDS or are on
        cocaine.

I hear the children crying
    all over the
        world.

I hear the children crying
    all over the
        world...

THE CHINESE REVOLUTION OF MAY, 1989
(THE YEAR OF THE SNAKE)

Over one million Chinese students are
    fasting and demonstrating for
    freedom and democracy . . .
the young, pale, earnest faces . . .
at first, they are treated medically and carefully . . .
the Government of the People's Republic of China
    and Washington D.C. are stunned.

Mikhail Gorbachev, who with his wife, Raisa, had
    wanted a summit of Peace with China, is
Bottlenecked from entering
Tianamen Square to shake hands with important
    dignitaries of the People's Republic of China . . .

Gorbachev has a calendar of speeches he has planned
    to impress the world...
The American Press is hailing him as an
    "EVANGELIST FOR PEACE."

Instead, he must shake hands at the airport . . .
he must wait two hours for the first appointment . . .

"Are there any more interruptions?" Gorbachev asks
    impatiently.

"Yes," say the leaders of the People's Republic of
    China.

After a banquet and several drinks of rice wine,
Gorbachev and Raisa go home . . .

Now, Tianamen Square is declared,
"THE SQUARE OF DISORDER" by the leaders of
the People's Republic of China.

The students are persuaded to stop the
    demonstration...
But the *people* of the People's Republic of China
will not allow it . . .
They block the roads to the Square
        so the trucks cannot get through.

MARTIAL LAW has been declared...
One leader resigns because he does not believe in
MARTIAL LAW...
It is rumored that he is under house arrest.

To the daughter of an immigrant to the
United States of America, it is a most thrilling sight—
There is *still* someone willing to die for
Democracy...
There is *still* someone willing to die for
Freedom!

No summit has taken place...
China remembers the Russian invasions of the past;
And Communism is a failure after all!

Meanwhile, Secretary of State, James Baker, is at
Kennebunkport, Maine,
Playing golf with the President of the United States of
    America, George Bush,

discussing the taking away of NATO
protection from Western Europe...

6:10 p.m., California time:
    All journalist transmission from
    Tianamen Square has now been
    cut . . .

THE BATTLE OF ARMAGEDDON
August 3, 1990

The Battle of Armageddon has begun in the Middle
   East.
As President George Bush says, "Someone has drawn
   a line in the sand."
The ancient land of Babylon, Iraq,
Has taken over oil-rich Kuwait.

Ancient Babylon, once ruled by King Nebucchadnezzar
(the "head of gold" in the Daniel prophecy),
Worshipped the sun-god, whose name is Marduk:
Ancient Babylon built the Tower of Babel,
Trying to reach the realm of Marduk,
In consequence of which,
Almighty God divided the languages
To cause confusion among men.

Ancient Babylon sacrificed its children to the sun
On the tops of ziggurats;
Old King Nebucchadnezzar went mad
And was forced to graze on grass like an ox.

His kingdom was taken from him in one night
By the Medes and the Persians
Because his son dared to use the vessels of the Holy
   Temple of Israel In his orgies.

Iraq's present leader has threatened to poke out the
Eyes of those who oppose Iraq . . .

We have sent 250,000 troops to Saudi Arabia in order
to Defend Saudi Arabia's borders...

Is Saudi Arabia our friend?
Saudi Arabia fought against Israel in the
SIX-DAY WAR . . .

This war will go all the way to Israel:
"There will soon be a great
Shaking in the land of Israel."

Meanwhile, the coasts of the U.S.A. will be drilled for
    oil and,
As the Bible says, some day,
"There will be no more sea."

"THE MARK OF THE BEAST"

West Germany has changed the currency of
  East Germany into
"Deutchmarks"—
This is the Beastmark, mentioned in the Bible—

After the Battle of Armageddon, Adolf Hitler, whose
  name is Satan,
Will bring the ten European Countries
("The Holy Roman Empire")
Against us in a nuclear Holocaust
(World War III).

"A stone cut without hands"
(Jesus Christ of Nazareth)
Will break the Nazi iron from the
Israeli clay in the feet of the monster mentioned in
  the Daniel prophecy.

"That stone will become a great mountain which will
  fill the whole earth...
Of His Kingdom there will be no end."

Your Social Security number and the numbers on your
Credit cards are part of
"The Mark of the Beast."

Jesus of Nazareth had no Social Security Number . . .
He had no home . . .
He was
Homeless.

He hid in the woods from the
Roman soldiers with his twelve
Disciples . . .

He was old and
Ill
Long before his
Time.

Your Social Security number and other
Numbers will be placed in
The Beast Computer in
Brussels, Belgium...Its number is
666...

Records will be kept on nearly
Everyone in the world,
So that people's intimate habits are known . . .
So that you can be
Blackmailed by the
Nazis.

Jesus of Nazareth was a
"Non-person,"
Who lived upon the earth . . .
He followed the Will of Almighty God and
He Conquered Death.

He had one robe, which the
Roman soldiers divided when he was on the
Cross.

He had one pair of
Sandals.

He told his disciples to take one
Cloak and one pair of
Sandals with them when they went out to
Preach.

He told them to wait in the Upper Room to
    receive
The Baptism of the Holy Ghost before they went
Out to preach...

How many of our present-day Sunday pastors
Have waited in the Upper Room?

Jesus kept the Commandments and the Jewish
Feast Days and honored the
Sabbath.

Jesus is
Jewish.

King Constantine changed the Jewish Holy Days to
Satisfy the Pagans.

His spiritual descendants are the False
Prophet
(The Pope—both East and West).
The Popes pretend they can forgive your sins for
    money.
They pretend they are God.

The Beast of the Apocalypse will use his shuttle
Diplomacy to bring about a false
Peace in the Middle East . . .

As the Bible says, in the middle of that seven-year
Treaty, it will be broken, and a nuclear
Holocaust will descend upon the
Earth . . .

Jesus of Nazareth's great Rapture will occur before
  that time.

THE FUNNY MAN

He calls himself,
"A funny man" . . .
He writes his letters on
Discarded Christmas papers of
Green or red or
Blue . . .

He calls himself just
"A funny man."

C O L O P H O N

This book is one of an edition of
six hundred fifty copies
printed and bound at The Golden Quill Press,
in the year nineteen-hundred ninety-one.
The text is set in a digital facsimile
of a typeface designed in 1540 by
Geofroy Tory's pupil, Claude Garamond,
on command of Francois I of France.
The text paper, Smyth-sewn in sixteen page signatures,
is Mohawk Mills' sixty-pound basis acid-free
Mohawk Cream White Vellum, manufactured at
Cohoes, New York.

This infinity symbol ∞
represents Golden Quill's commitment to quality paper stock,
which will last several centuries,
and our cooperation with
The National Information Standards Organization, Washington, DC.